SCOTT MATTHEWS

# SERIOUSLY PUNNY

# 101 SILLY PUNS, JOKES & HILARIOUS WORDPLAY

Puns are the perfect mix of wordplay, humor, and a little bit of groaning. They've been around for thousands of years, from ancient texts to today's memes, and they're all about playing with words that sound alike or have double meanings.

But what exactly makes them so irresistible?

# Language Quirks

Puns thrive on homophones (words that sound the same but mean different things) and homonyms (words with multiple meanings), which makes language a playground for punsters.

# Our Love for Double Meanings

Puns surprise us. That "aha!" moment when a word takes on a new meaning is what makes them so satisfying—and often hilarious.

# Historical Roots

Puns aren't new! They've been used in ancient Egyptian texts, Greek plays, and even Shakespeare's works, where he dropped over 3,000 puns.

# Brain Wiring

Our brains are wired to spot patterns and make connections, so puns exploit that tendency, giving us a little twist that keeps us on our toes.

Puns are born from language's quirks and our brain's love for cleverness—a timeless recipe for laughter.

# Ready to dive deeper into the world of puns?

Why did the cookie cry? Because his father was a wafer so long!

I used to work in a shoe recycling shop. It was sole-destroying.

There's a new type of broom out; it's sweeping the nation.

Whiteboards are remarkable.

I took a vacation
in the Arctic.
Cool trip.

I wanted to be a history teacher...
But there's no future in it.
HISTORY CLASS

I accidentally glued myself
to my autobiography.
That's my story, and I'm sticking to it.
MY LIFE

I met a skeleton
at a party.
He had no body to
dance with.

My friend wants to become an archaeologist,
but life's just too much of a dig right now.

My plane joke
didn't land.

What do you call an
alligator in a vest?
An investigator.

Why are cats so good at
video games?
Because they have nine lives.
REVIVE?

I told my curtains we
needed space.
They drew themselves shut.

What do cows tell each other
at bedtime?
Dairy tales.

Why do bees have sticky hair?
Because they use honeycombs.

Why did the grape stop in the middle of the road?
It ran out of juice.
REST AREA

I dated **someone from the library.**
We had too many issues.

I tried to start a hot sauce company,
but I couldn't handle the heat.
HOT
SAUCE

I named my dog "Coffee" because he always grounds me.

Want to hear a pizza joke?
Never mind, it's too cheesy.

# I once dated an artist,
### but he just painted me in a bad light.

I lost my remote.
Now everything's out
of control.

DELIVERY
CHICKEN
EGG
I ordered a chicken and an egg.
I'll let you know what comes first.

I wanted to be an astronaut, but my career never took off.

I wanted to be a historian,
but I just couldn't get
past the present.
HISTORY
HISTORY
HISTORY
HISTORY
HISTORY
HISTORY
PRESENT DAY

What's a pirate's
favorite subject?
Arrrrt.

I walked into a travel agency and asked about time travel.
They said, "You're early."

# Why didn't the lion win the race?
## Because he was racing a cheetah.

The stapler is the most well-attached office supply.

The scissors and I
had a falling out.
Things got a
bit snippy.

I don't trust stairs.
They're always up to something.

I once had a job as a
human statue,
but I just couldn't stand it.

BANK
I quit my job
as a banker;
it just didn't
make cents.

Why did the octopus beat the shark in a fight?
Because it was well armed.

# The elevator business has its ups and downs.

# What did one hat say to the other?

Stay here, I'm going on ahead.

I dated a locksmith once.
She had the key to my heart.

I drove my car into
a tree yesterday.
Now I'm really stumped.

I'd tell you a joke
about trains,
but it might go off the rails.
JOKE BOOK

I tried to eat
a clock.
It was time-consuming.

I tried writing with a
broken pencil...
But it was pointless.

# I once ate a dictionary.

It gave me thesaurus throat ever.

I just burned 2,000 calories.
I forgot the pizza in the oven.

THINK
OUTSIDE
THE BOX
Claustrophobic
people are more
productive
thinking outside
the box.

What do you call a
cow with no legs?
Ground beef.

I wrote a song
about tortillas...
But it's a little flat.

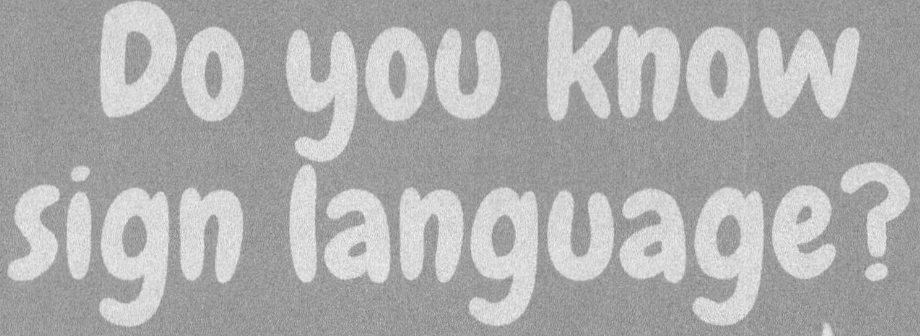

Do you know sign language?
You should learn it: it's pretty handy.

What do you call a sheep covered in chocolate?
A candy baa.

# The accountant broke up with his calculator.

He felt like he was just another number.

I saw a
chicken
at the gym.
It was working
on its pecks.

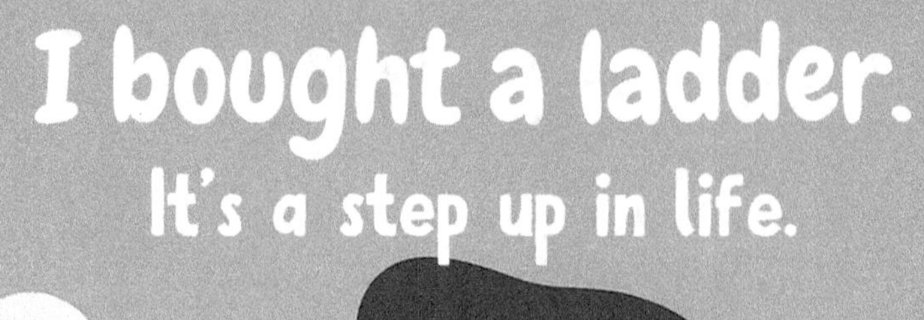


I bought a ladder.
It's a step up in life.

I got promoted to head of
staplers.
It was a binding decision.
HEAD OF STAPL

CAMOUFLAGE PANTS
?
I bought camouflage pants,
but I can't find them.

The math teacher called me obtuse.
I said, "That's not right."

BUSINESS
CEO-YO
I started a company
making yoyos...
It has its ups and downs.

My cat was
just sick on
the carpet,
I don't think
it's feline well.

# My mirror got dramatic.

Now it's reflecting on everything.

What do you call a group of
musical whales?
An orca-stra.

# I went to Egypt,
### but it was all just a pyramid scheme.

I told my plants I love them.
Now I'm rooted in commitment.

I built a model of Mount Everest.
It's a high point in my life.

O
Au
The periodic table's parties are pretty elementary.

I adopted a snail. We're bonding, but it's taking things slow.

I made a belt out
of sausages.
It was a waist of meat.

I tried working at a
blanket factory,
but I got covered in work.

My job at the calendar factory was short-lived.
I took a few days off.
MISSING

The moon threw a party, but no one came.
Guess it needed more space.

Why did the student bring a ladder to class?
To go to high school.

I made a pun about
a balloon....
It popped off.

How do you organize an
outer space party?
You planet.

I broke up with my fridge.
It was too cold.

MONTH
I had abs once.
Now they're just...
ab-sent.

I told my date she had a great sense of direction.
She left.
EXIT

I was gonna end this list with a joke about paper, but it's tearable.

That peanut
butter was
so good.
It was nuts.
PEANUT
BUTTER

My washing machine
ghosted me.
It just stopped spinning
me around.

I work at a paper factory.
It's a real sheet show.

I quit my janitor job.
The job was sweeping me away.

Do you know where you can get chicken broth in bulk?
The stock market.
BROTH ↑
BROTH
BROTH

I named my printer
Bob Marley,
because it's always jammin'.

I got hired at a shoelace company.
I'm tied up at the moment.

I opened a GPS company.
I needed some direction in life.
N
W
E
S

Why did the student bring a flashlight to class?
To brighten their future.

I dated a candle once.
It burned out.

I bought a cloak of invisibility.
I can't find it now.

I told a joke about unemployment,
but it never worked.

I tried to sell my vacuum,
but it sucked too much to keep.

I used to sell bonsai trees.
It was my "small business."
SHOP

What's the difference between a well-dressed man on a bicycle and a badly dressed man on a tricycle? Attire.

I started a memory club...
But we keep forgetting to meet.
MEETING TODAY?

I don't know what happened
to my imaginary friend.
He ghosted me.

I tried to make a pun
about infinity....
But it never ends.

I put my root beer in a square cup.
Now it's just beer.

I put my phone in
airplane mode.
It took off without me.

It was an emotional wedding.
Even the cake had tiers.

# Why did the dog sit in the shade?

Because it didn't want to be a hot dog.

One bird can't
make a pun.
But toucan.
PUN
INTENDED
?

I started talking
to my blender.
It really mixed things up.

I made a pun about maps,
but it didn't go anywhere.

My math teacher called me average.
How mean!
MEAN
MEDIAN
AVERAGE

# The stars started a union.
## They were tired of working night shifts.

Did you hear about the guy who lost the left side of his body?
He's alright now.

The elevator and I have a
complicated relationship;
it always lets me down.
OUT
ORDER

BREAKUP
LETTER

The Moon broke up
with Earth;
it said it needed space.

The microwave started dating the toaster, talk about a heated relationship.